The Earth Strikes Back

How we use and abuse our planet

LAND

Arthur Haswell

Chrysalis Children's Books

First published in Great Britain in 2000 by
Chrysalis Children's Books
An imprint of Chrysalis Books Group Plc
The Chrysalis Building, Bramley Road, London W10 6SP

Paperback edition first published in 2004

Editor Claire Edwards
Designer Helen James
Picture researcher Kathy Lockley
Illustrator William Donohoe
Consultant Chris Baines

ISBN 1 84138 040 7 (hardback)
ISBN 1 84138 942 0 (paperback)

British Library Cataloguing in Publication Data
for this book is available from the British Library.

Printed in China

Words in **bold** are explained in the glossary on pages 30 and 31.

Picture acknowledgements
Environmental Images / Vanessa Mills 36 B, /Robert Brook 31 T
Sally & Richard Greenhill 11 T
Robert Harding Picture Library , 24 T, 24 B, 25 B, 26, 28 B, 41 T
Hutchison Library /Trevor Page 40 T, / 18 T, /Isabella Tree 15 T, /T. Molins 7
Frank Lane Picture Agency /W Broadhurst 32, 35 T, 40 B, 41 B, /Silvestris 36 T, /Chris Demefriou 9 T, /Leo Batten 16
Magnum /© Fred Mayer 29, /© Steve McCurry 18 B
Ted Mead 23 B, 34 B
Peter Newark's Pictures 14 T
Panos Pictures /Ray Wood 44, /Jeremy Hartley 45, /Howard David 27 T, 31 B, / © Sean Sprague 17 B, /Neil Cooper 21 B
Rex Features 8, 28 T
Russia & Republics Photolibrary 33
Science Photo Library /David Thurber/AGSTOCK 13 B, /Dr Morley Read 10 T, / Ed Young/AGSTOCK 6 T /Lowell Georgia 11 B, /Martin Land 6 B, /Russ Munn/AGSTOCK 17 T, /Simon Yerrey 3, 9 B, /Worldsat International & J. Knighton 4 T
Frank Spooner Pictures 30
Still Pictures / 35, /Nigel Dickinson 34 T, /Mark Edwards 20 B, 25 T, 27 B, /Fredy Mercay 22 B, /Hillier Mason 22 T, /John Maier 13 T, /Jorgen Schytte 19 T, /M & C Denis-Huot 20 T, /Mark Edwards 12, 19 B, 21 T, /Martin Hawes 5, /Shezad Nooran 15 B
Steven C. Wilson/ENTHEOS 14 B
WWF-UK /Clive James Hicks 23 T

Contents

Planet Earth

About one third of the Earth's surface is land. Humans live on the land, sharing it with plants and animals. But the land is changing all the time.

▲ *From space, land on Earth forms green and brown patches in a sea of blue.*

When Earth began

Our planet began as a fiery ball of gas, with a core of molten rock. As the surface cooled, it formed a crust. The landmasses on Earth today are based on rocks about 3500 million years old.

These landmasses (continents) have moved around the planet, floating on molten rock, called **magma**. About 500 million years ago there were only four continents. These came together to form a single supercontinent called Pangaea. Then, about 175 million years ago, Pangaea broke up, and the continents we see today began to move to their present positions. They are still moving now.

▼ *This diagram shows how Pangaea divided to create our modern continents.*

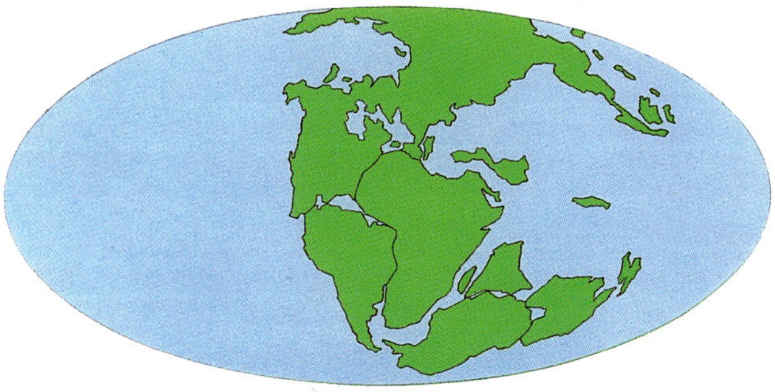

225 million years ago

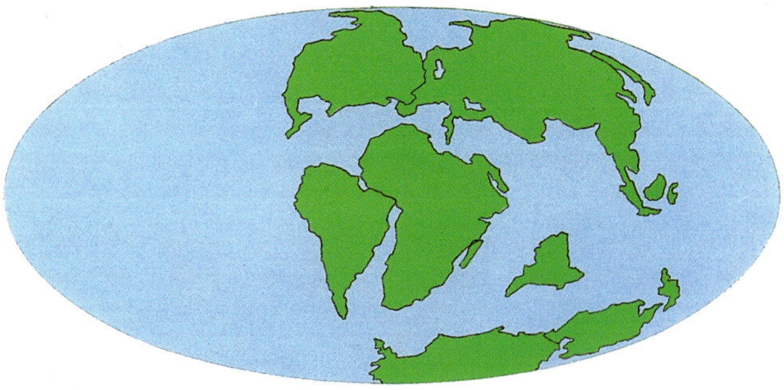

135 million years ago

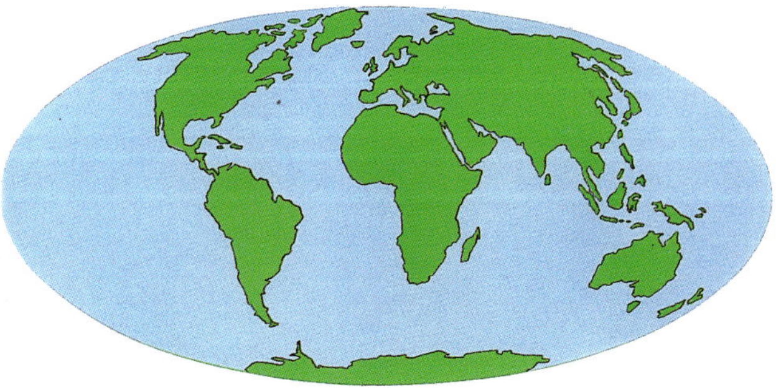

The present

▲ *Wilderness areas, such as this river estuary in Tasmania, are areas of land that have been unaltered by humans. They are often protected by law from change.*

When humans arrived

Tens of thousands of years ago most land was covered in an untouched **wilderness** of forests and natural vegetation. By about 1500 BC the first farmers had cleared small patches of land to grow food and to build villages. The removal of Earth's natural covering of plants, which had thrived for millions of years, had begun. It has never stopped.

Earth's land area has hardly changed since the times of our earliest ancestors, but the number of people living on it has changed dramatically. Only 2000 years ago the world population was a mere 200 million. Now the same area of land is home to 6000 million people. Most of us will never see land that has been unshaped or untouched by humans.

Making peace with our planet

The forces that created the land and that are still changing it are beyond our control. Humans have little power compared with the molten rock inside our planet, the rain, snow, wind and sun. But we do affect our planet just by living. A single person may not change things much, but large groups can destroy natural systems. With modern technology we are changing the land by farming it, mining it, building on it and polluting it. Will the land still provide food and homes for people in the future? We must work to repair people's damage, and learn to live in harmony with our **environment**.

Land and us

The first life on Earth began in the oceans. About 500 million years ago, plants and animals began to adapt to life on land. Humans, who have developed within the last five million years, can live only on land.

▲ *These neat rows of cabbages stretch into the distance. This crop will provide food for thousands of people.*

Adaptable people

As people have spread over the planet they have learned to live in many different environments, from hot deserts to icy wastes, from mountain villages to coastal **plains**. Few species have so successfully covered the available land on Earth.

▼ *Precious stones, such as this opal, are cut and polished to be used in jewellery. Gemstones are formed from rocks.*

Land for resources

Human effect on the land has increased as people have learned to use more and more of its **natural resources**. Early people discovered how to make fire. This allowed them to cook and keep warm, and later to work with molten metals.

Land provides the **raw materials** of almost everything we use in our every day lives. Life without its products is difficult to imagine. How could we live without crops grown on land, wood from trees, and dairy products from grazing animals? Land is also the source of **minerals** and metals, stone, and **fossil fuels** such as coal and oil.

Land for leisure

Millions of people like to visit areas of great natural beauty for pleasure. Organizations and governments have responded to this by preserving natural landscapes wherever they can – from vast national reserves to small town parks. There are areas of cliffs, seashore, mountains, rivers and wilderness, where people can enjoy outdoor activities without harming the environment.

My land, your land

Who decides whether a plot of natural land is ploughed for wheat, mined for minerals, or left untouched? Who owns the wilderness? In Australia the Aborigines lived off vast areas of land for thousands of years without ploughing or mining. But when European settlers arrived they claimed the land as their own, believing that only legal documents prove ownership. Now mining companies want to dig up the Australian wilderness. Local Aborigines say the land is theirs and should not be mined, and judges and politicians will have to decide who really owns the land.

► *As climbing becomes a more and more popular sport, there is a danger that cliffs and mountains will be affected. Climbers are encouraged to follow rules so that they do not damage the rock face.*

The land cycle

Land is constantly changing. New parts form while others wear away. Sometimes we are reminded of this, as a cliff falls into the sea. But usually the land changes too slowly for us to notice.

▲ *In Monument Valley, USA, softer rock has been worn away, leaving towers of harder rocks in what was once a higher landscape.*

Earth's skin

The Earth's crust varies in thickness from 80 kilometres under the highest mountains, to 6 kilometres under some areas of the ocean. It is divided into huge pieces called plates, which float on a layer of hot rock called the mantle. The mantle is partly made up of magma (molten rock), which puts the crust under constant pressure. Changes to the Earth's crust happen at the edges of the plates.

Making mountains

When two plates carrying land move towards one another, the edge of one is pushed down below the other. The crust from one plate slides back into the mantle, while the crust of the other crumples upwards and outwards to form hills and fold mountains. The movement of plates may also cause huge cracks, called faults, in the rocks. Pressure in the magma may force up a block of land between two faults, or a block may slip down between the faults. This creates block mountains.

▼ *Mountains form over hundreds of millions of years, and are gradually eroded.*

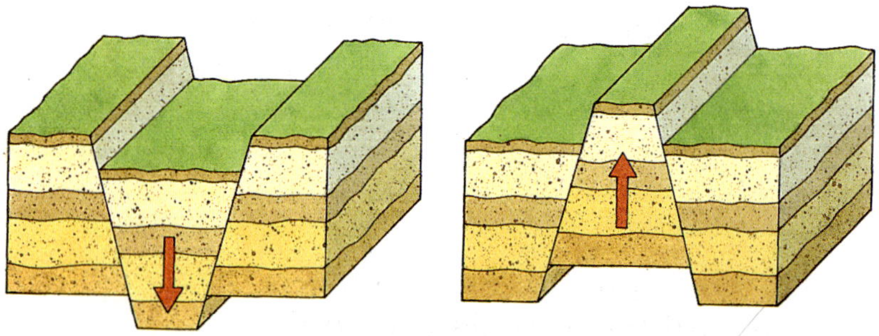

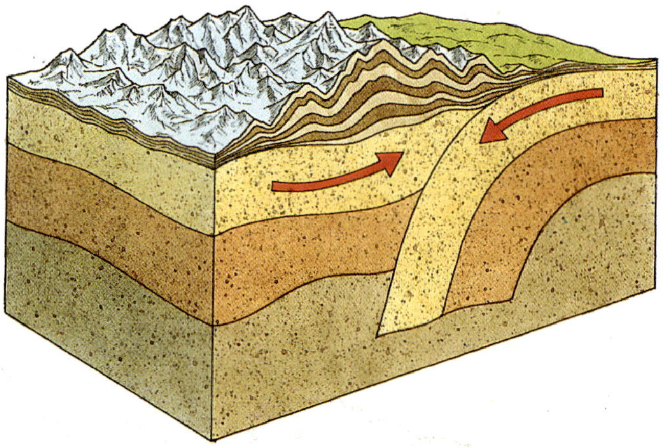

Earth's rocks

The Earth's crust is formed from three basic types of rock. **Igneous rock** is cooled magma from the mantle. **Sedimentary rock** was formed in layers under water as sand, mud, dead plants and even tiny animals sank to the bottom of ancient seas, rivers and lakes. (Coal is formed from plants that grew in swamps millions of years ago.) **Metamorphic rock** is formed by changes in igneous or sedimentary rock. For instance pressure and heat change sedimentary limestone into marble.

▲ *Moving water, such as this waterfall, cuts into rock, forming valleys.*

Wearing land away

These rocks form the mountains and all the land we walk on. But just as mountains are being formed, they are also constantly being worn away. Wind and water rush over the land, carrying grit and stones that batter the surface. Water freezing and thawing in cracks, and dramatic changes in temperature all break up the rock. Plant roots also grow down into rocks, widening cracks and helping to break up the rock. These changes, together with rainfall, are part of a natural process called **weathering**. Weathering wears away softer rocks first, leaving behind areas of more resistant rock.

▼ *This cliff face is a time machine. Clay left by melting ice lies on red sandstone laid down when this land was a desert.*

Soil systems

Soil is made up of tiny pieces of rock, dead and living plants and animals, water and air. Nature takes at least 200 years to create a good soil, in which plants and animals thrive.

▲ *This unprotected soil has turned to mud and been baked hard by the sun.*

The parent rock

A soil has many layers, from fallen leaves on top, through the richest middle layers, down to the **parent rock**. The greatest part of a soil comes from the parent rock, including the minerals on which plants feed. The parent rock affects how acid the soil is and what plants grow there. For instance, the alkaline soil on limestone supports different plants from those growing in the acid soil of granite rock.

Different dirt

Not all soils have the same structure. The size of rock **particles** is very important. Loose, sandy soil with large particles has plenty of air, but does not hold water well. Very sandy soil in dry areas can turn to dust which is picked up and blown around by the wind. Vegetation cannot grow, and desert begins to form.

Tiny clay particles hold water much better, but do not drain well. If clay absorbs lots of water it forms a sticky mass. But when clay dries out it shrinks and becomes hard like concrete. Plants find it difficult to spread their roots through this soil.

◄ *This cross section shows plants and burrowing animals in a healthy, fertile soil.*

Fertile soil

Plant roots bind the soil and stop it being washed or blown away. As plants die, their roots, leaves and stems **decay** to create **humus**. This improves soil texture so the soil can store more water. It also provides **nitrogen** and other food for living plants. Tunnels made by creatures such as earthworms and ants help water and air to enter the soil. Other creatures that live in the soil range from moles and shrews to microscopic **bacteria** that change the **compost** of dead matter into food for the next generation of plants.

Well-balanced soils that support life are called fertile soils. They hold enough rain and **nutrients** to feed plants, while being light enough to allow excess water to drain away.

The fastest soil on Earth

Loess is a light soil made up of soil dust blown from deserts and laid down in a new place. It builds up to form a very fertile soil. In central China the loess **plateau** (below) is hundreds of metres thick and people have dug homes into its side. Rice is grown in this rich soil to feed China's huge population. But rain can quickly form deep gullies, and carry the soil away.

▼ *Dust storms, such as this one in Georgia, USA, strip dry soil from the land.*

Clearing the land

People clear land of wild vegetation to make room to build homes and to grow food. They also use this vegetation to burn as fuel, or for building material.

In the clear

One traditional way of using land, especially in tropical forests, is for shifting cultivation. Tribal people clear a small area (about a hectare) of forest. They plant crops such as maize and sweet potatoes. They also add to their diet by hunting animals and gathering food growing wild in the forest. The soil will only support their crops for two or three years, then the people clear a new area. The area they leave behind takes about 50 years to return to its natural state. In vast forests, such small areas do little harm to the land or wildlife.

▲ *The Yanomami prepare land in the Amazon rainforest for growing vegetables.*

Slash and burn

Growing populations and the demand for more farmland means that land is being cleared at a faster rate than ever before. Natural plants, including forests, are being cut down all over the world to clear land for farming. The simplest way to clear land is to slash down the plants and burn them. In Madagascar 83 per cent of the original forest cover has been removed by slash and burn, to provide land for **cash crops** and local food production. Unless this stops, only areas of steeply sloping land is likely to remain forested.

▲ *Forest fires are used to clear large areas of natural forest every year.*

Thinning trees

Cutting down wood for fuel, paper, building materials and furniture is called logging. Logging has cleared forests all over the world. In Europe only one per cent of natural forest survives. In the last 40 years Asia has lost 40 per cent of its forests.

▼ *Modern farming often uses vast areas of land to grow a single crop, as on this cotton farm.*

Planting trees

All over the world trees are being grown in plantations, or sustainable forests. Each consists of just one or two, fast-growing types of tree. These provide very poor natural **habitats** for other plants and animals, but they do produce wood without harming natural forests.

A changing landscape

As the demand for food grows, huge fields are planted with single crops. Hedgerows are cut down, and other plants are killed with chemicals. The natural habitat with its variety of plants and animals is gradually destroyed. In some countries, new laws encourage farmers to save hedges, so that modern farmland still offers a home for wildlife.

Stripped soil

Over the years, wind and water may destroy soil, by blowing or washing it away. This is called erosion. But people often cause the worst soil erosion.

▲ *In the 1930s many farms, like this one in South Dakota, USA, were covered in dry soil blown off the land in the dustbowl.*

Lonely loess

In Tennessee, USA, natural vegetation that once covered the soil was cleared from vast areas of loess hills to allow modern machines to farm the fertile land. Now, only a few years later, much of the loess soil has gone. Here and there a tree has bound the soil together, and appears perched above the lifeless ground.

The Dust Bowl

The vast plains of North America once had a natural covering of grass and wild plants. Native Americans knew how to live off this land, but when farmers in the 1930s ploughed it and planted wheat, they ran into problems. The roots of the wheat were too short to bind the soil or to hold enough moisture. Winds blew the soil away and created a desert that they called the Dust Bowl. Soil **erosion** is still a major problem worldwide. Some scientists think that it may have destroyed as much as 33 per cent of the world's cropland over the past 40 years.

◄ *In this barren landscape, the land used to be at the level of this tree. When the other trees were felled, the loess was quickly eroded by wind and rain.*

Washed away

Many rivers begin in forest-covered hills and mountains. When rain falls it is taken up by tree roots, or held in the soil, and released into the rivers gradually. But where forests have been felled, the soil is easily blown or washed away, allowing rainwater to run straight into the rivers.

For centuries people living in what is now Bangladesh have relied on the annual **monsoon** to bring heavy rains. The rain swells the rivers that run down from the foothills of the Himalayas. The flood water enriches the soil and restocks **groundwater** for drinking. But over the last 40 years half the trees in the mountains have been cut down. In 1998 the rivers flooded more than ever before, destroying rice crops and cows. This caused severe food shortages.

Trees and terraces

A good way of preventing soil erosion on farmlands is to grow trees among the crops, to keep the soil fertile and hold it in place. This has always been done in Bali, Indonesia. On hills and mountains, water erosion can be reduced by cutting the slope into level terraces, to slow the flow of water. Rice is often grown in this way.

▼ *Workers in Dhaka, Bangladesh, make their way home through the 1998 floods.*

Starving soil

Plants feed on nutrients in soil. On land untouched by humans these nutrients are provided mainly by wild plants as they grow, die and decay in one place. But when land is cleared, the nutrients are no longer replaced.

Overworking the soil

The ancient Romans used land in North Africa to grow their wheat. The wheat took up nutrients from the soil as it grew. It was then cut and sent away. After a while there were no nutrients left in the soil, and plants could not grow. Eventually the area became part of the Sahara Desert.

Giving land a rest

For thousands of years farmers in Europe used a three-field system. In one field they grew wheat or rye, in another peas or beans, while the third was not planted but left fallow. The following year the

▼ *Sometimes farmland is allowed to rest, allowing wild plants to nourish the soil.*

▲ *Maize plants take lots of nitrogen from the soil. Farmers do not allow the soil to rest, but plant maize every year and apply nitrogen-rich fertilizer.*

system would move round, allowing each field to recover for one year in three. Farmers discovered that they could also improve the soil by adding bones and rotting plants to their fields. These were the first fertilizers.

Factory made

Most modern farmers cannot afford to allow land to lie fallow. They use **artificial fertilizers** to feed the soil. These contain all the chemicals plants need to grow. Over the last 50 years the use of these fertilizers worldwide has increased tenfold. In the USA, farmers who used to harvest less than two tonnes of corn per hectare now reap nearly eight tonnes. But although artificial fertilizers help to produce larger crops, they are expensive and can harm wildlife. They may also have a long-term harmful effect on the soil.

Human waste

Throughout history, human sewage has been used to fertilize fields. Artificial fertilizers were introduced in **developed countries** about 100 years ago, but became more common after the First World War. In other parts of the world the old system continues. The Chinese transport human sewage from cities to the countryside by rail. The SIRDO system, recently developed in Mexico, uses sunshine to convert human sewage into fertilizer that can be sold to local farms. Such a simple, cheap way of using a resource available everywhere, could produce the fertilizers of the future.

Expanding deserts

Deserts make up a third of the Earth's land surface. Many people live at the desert edge, where the land is more fertile. But even here the land is fragile and easily damaged.

▲ *Large cattle herds are stripping the savannah in southern Sudan, Africa, turning fragile land to desert.*

Salty soil

Some people develop **irrigation** systems in an attempt to grow crops in desert areas. But watering ground that receives little rain can cause problems. If too much water is taken for irrigation, the vegetation and soil around the water's natural source may be destroyed. If the land is not drained properly the sun evaporates the water, drawing salty underground water to the surface. As this water evaporates, the salt builds up on the surface, making the land infertile.

▼ *Dry soil and sand from the Sahara Desert is blown on the wind to cover crops and houses.*

The stretching Sahara

The Sahara is one of the driest places on Earth, where little can survive. Around its edge there is enough water for scattered trees and vegetation to grow, and for people to farm in a delicate balance with the land. But over the last 20 years the southern edge of the Sahara Desert has crept south by 100 kilometres. Some of this spread is natural, but human activity has made it worse.

As huge areas of crops have been planted south of the desert, local people have been forced closer to the desert and crowded into areas too small for their herds. The cows have eaten the vegetation that once kept the soil fertile. Their hoofs have turned the soil to dust. This has been eroded by the wind and rain, making the land infertile.

▲ *In Africa, women and children usually collect wood for fires and stoves. As more wood is taken, they have to travel further every day.*

Securing the sand

Dusty soil is easily blown away by the wind, but some plants have roots that help to hold it in place. In Niger acacia trees have been planted to stop wind erosion. The trees have taproots that burrow deep underground to reach moisture and smaller roots that fan out to collect rain. In Somalia local people have planted brushwood on sand dunes. These bushes look dead at first, but they send out roots when rain falls, stabilizing the sand dunes and allowing other plants to grow.

Wood for fire

About half of the world's population still burns firewood for cooking and heat, but around many deserts there are few trees left. The loss of trees has increased soil erosion, and people have to walk further to find fuel. In Kenya, women have set up The Green Belt Movement, where communities grow young trees to plant. Across Africa 35 countries have set up similar projects.

Tropical rainforest

Tropical rainforests grow in countries around the Equator, such as Brazil, the Congo and Indonesia. Rainforests cover about seven per cent of land on Earth, but an area almost the size of England is being cut down every year.

▲ *This golden bamboo lemur is one of many species found in the wild only in Madagascar's shrinking rainforest. There are only 400 left in the world.*

The living forest

The tallest trees in the rainforest provide a roof of branches 50 metres up called a canopy. This keeps out direct sunlight, and stops heat escaping. Underneath, the air is warm and damp, ideal for bacteria and fungi. Half the world's species of plants and animals live there, and many can be found nowhere else.

▼ *People in the Cameroons earn money by collecting plants from the forest for traditional healers to make into medicines.*

Farming failures

Although tropical forests look very fertile, their soil is actually quite thin. But the combination of high rainfall and temperatures makes the **organisms** in the soil very active, so that plants grow, die and decay quickly. This creates a shallow layer of humus at the surface, which provides the nutrients that keep the forest alive. When the land is cleared, this layer is washed away by the rain. Attempts to farm crops on the land usually fail because the soil underneath is too poor, and the sun bakes the unprotected soil hard so that plants cannot grow.

▲ *Cattle graze on land that used to be rainforest in Brazil. A few years of farming cattle for beef are usually enough to exhaust the thin soil.*

Timber!

Furniture made from forest trees such as teak and mahogany is very popular in developed countries, especially Japan and USA. When loggers cut down these trees, other trees around them are damaged by the heavy machinery. Only about 40 per cent of each log is used. Loggers also prefer to clear-fell, which means that they cut down everything, and take only what they want. The land can then be used to graze cattle, or is often given to poor farmers who try to grow crops on it.

At present, 12 million hectares of rainforest are cleared each year. At this rate the world's rainforest will disappear within 60 years. But governments are beginning to realize that rainforests are too valuable to lose, and are taking steps to protect by law the forests that are left.

Temperature tamers

Tropical rainforests affect everyone on Earth because they are so vast. As sunlight falls on the trees, the leaves release water, which forms high clouds. Some of these are blown towards cooler lands all over the world, making the weather there warmer and less severe. The trees and plants also take in **carbon dioxide** through their leaves to help them grow, and release oxygen. In this way they reduce carbon dioxide in the atmosphere, and help to combat **global warming**.

Wetlands

About a quarter of the world's different types of plant grow in wetlands. They cover six per cent of land, providing homes for more than half our fish, and resting places for migrating birds.

Wetlands exist around the world's coastlines, and along rivers that regularly flood. They range from bogs and marshes to flooded forests and shallow lakes, and provide a unique habitat. Because wetlands are not ideally suited for building on they have been partly protected for many years. But until recently their value has not been truly appreciated.

▲ *The star-shaped roots are all that remain of this cleared mangrove forest.*

Guarding the coast

Wetlands around tropical coasts are home to mangroves. These plants can live in salty water or in airless, waterlogged mud. Roots grow from the trunk, supporting it above the water, and the tangle of roots holds debris and soil. Forests of mangroves protect coasts from sea erosion and flooding. They provide a clean, sheltered home for fish and shellfish to breed in. Local communities rely on mangrove habitats for fishing, but large areas have been cleared to provide firewood, or have been destroyed by soil erosion or **pollution** from sewage and oil spills.

◀ *Mangroves are a type of wetland rainforest. The trees grow above the water on thick roots and the habitat this provides is teeming with life.*

Looking after wetlands

The aim of the world's first **conservation treaty**, signed in 1971, was to protect wetlands. Since then nearly 800 sites have been listed all over the world. In China many wetlands have been threatened by drainage, and plans to build dams. Now the Chinese government, working with the Asian Wetland Bureau and the Worldwide Fund for Nature, are putting together an action plan to preserve wetland areas such as the one shown below.

Marshes or farms

About half of the wetlands in the USA have been drained. Farmland has been created, but unique marshes have been lost. Around parts of the coast, land that was once covered by the tide twice a day is now covered by houses.

Many wetlands occur where great rivers enter the sea. They rely on **sediment** carried by the rivers to build up layers of mud. But dams built on the Mississippi River have reduced the amount of sediment, so the marshes around the Mississippi Delta in Louisiana are shrinking by 100 square kilometres a year. The Wetlands Reserve Program was set up in 1990. It aims to restore areas of marshes that have been drained.

▼ *Magela Creek Wetlands, in Australia, though protected, are in danger from uranium mining that could poison the land.*

Growing cities

Today almost half of the world's population lives in cities, and that number is rising. Cities take over farm land and create huge amounts of waste and pollution.

▲ *Modern cities, such as Tokyo, spread over vast areas of land once used for farming.*

Losing land

As the world population rises, there is an increasing problem housing everyone. Every week more people arrive or are born into the world's cities, which now cover twice as much land as they did 20 years ago. For example, in Denver, USA, 90 000 acres of prime farmland disappears every year as new houses are built, and new roads allow people to drive into the city for work or shopping.

Suburban sprawl

Cities in developing countries are growing especially quickly. São Paulo is the biggest city in Brazil and every year another half a million people go to live there. About 20 per cent of the population live in slums or shanty towns, called *favelas*, round the edges of the city. People build shacks from anything they can find.

◄ *Cities are areas of poverty and of economic growth. This shanty town is in São Paulo, Brazil. The rich modern city can be seen in the distance.*

▲ *New York's Fresh Kills landfill site on Staten island can be seen from space.*

The shacks have no running water or toilets, and are crowded close together. In 1996 the United Nations recommended ways to improve life in *favelas*, for instance by setting up gardens where communities could grow fresh food, and by giving grants to local people to look after their own district.

What a lot of garbage!

USA's cities and towns produce more than 100 million tonnes of waste each day. In New York, the world's fourth largest city, dealing with rubbish is a major problem. Most of it is carried by boat to Staten Island, south of the main city, and dumped on the world's biggest **landfill**. Landfill sites are holes in the ground, where waste is squashed and covered with soil.

New life in inner cities

Over time city centres often become derelict. This may be because land in the centre becomes too expensive, or because industry fails. Liverpool was a great port until the decline of its shipping industry. Now its warehouses have been converted into shops, offices, and homes (below). Many cities are trying to improve housing in central districts and create a better environment, rather than expanding on to surrounding farmland.

Roads across the land

A new road changes the land it passes through. Today there are more than 500 million cars driving along the world's roads – ten times as many as there were 50 years ago. Shops and hotels are built around roads, and villages on main roads may grow into towns.

More cars, more roads

As populations grow, more people own cars, and more roads are built to take the extra traffic. In Britain many railway lines linking towns and villages were closed in the 1960s to save money. Now roads help people to reach more places. Ring roads are roads that take traffic around the edges of towns. They help to lessen pollution and traffic where people live. But as a result, countryside and farmland is destroyed and polluted.

Often when new roads are built through countryside the land around them is landscaped. Although the natural habitat is lost, these areas

▼ *Modern road junctions cover large areas of land, but the land around them can provide new wildlife habitats.*

▲ *In many countries people are forming local and national groups to protest against building roads across the countryside.*

do contain a wealth of wildlife. As fields have been turned over to **monoculture**, and towns have expanded, the land beside roads has begun to be valued, because it can provide a new wildlife habitat.

Road protesters

Because roads bring pollution and change to the land around them, many people are beginning to petition against the building of roads across unspoilt countryside. In the USA about half the national forests are crisscrossed with roads. Now people are asking the US government to ban the building of new roads in order to protect the forest.

Into the forest

The crowded cities of Brazil have grown up beside the Atlantic Ocean. Away from the coast there are vast areas of untouched land. For years the Brazilians wanted to exploit the minerals and other resources there, and move poor people out from the cities to become farmers.

In 1975 they completed the Trans-Amazonian Highway, which stretches 6400 kilometres across the middle of the country. This allowed settlers to move to freshly-cleared land. But many have failed to make a living from their new farms, because the soil is so poor. Large areas of forest are damaged and the traffic also causes pollution and kills animals.

▲ This Brazilian road will allow trucks to take away newly-felled trees and bring in new people to farm the cleared land.

Mining damage

The Earth provides us with fuel, metal and stone. But quarrying stone and mining for minerals on a huge scale can damage the land.

▲ *Many people were killed by landslides at the gold mine in Serra Pelada, Brazil, where the land had been dug away.*

Lasting effects

Mining has a long-term effect on the environment. In some parts of the world, you can still see where stone age people mined flints from the earth thousands of years ago.

Tunnelling underground

All round the world people still dig underground for coal and burn it to make electricity. Shafts are bored straight down, and tunnels run off them in **seams** of coal. Waste rock is brought up to the surface, and piled into huge waste heaps. The natural environment is destroyed, and the waste heaps can cause terrible local disasters.

▲ *Strip mining in South Africa has destroyed the coastal landscape and the creatures and plants that lived there.*

Biggest hole in the world

Open-cast mining strips rock from the surface to dig down and reach minerals. A road often spirals into the mine, so lorries can come and go. Huge areas of land are destroyed in this way. Digging began at the Bingham Canyon copper mine, USA, in 1906. Since then five billion tonnes of rock have been removed. Today the mine is 700 metres deep and covers more than seven square kilometres, and it is still growing.

The beautiful and the ugly

South Africa is rich in diamonds. Most are found deep underground, but some lie only 200 metres below the surface. Along the coast, strip miners bulldoze away the sand to reach the diamond-rich gravel below. Some people want the land restored, but others welcome the jobs and money that mining brings.

◄ *Bingham Canyon is an open-cast mine. It is the biggest man-made hole in the world and attracts 200 000 tourists every year.*

Restoring the land

Between 1993 and 1997, 180 000 tonnes of copper were taken from an open-cast mine in Wisconsin, USA. When mining stopped, the hole was partly refilled with mined rocks and then landscaped. Wetland plants were introduced. Now the area is a home for wildlife and migrating birds once more, as well as a place for tourists to visit.

Poisoning the land

Many industries, factories and power stations produce dangerous chemical waste. Disposing of this waste can have a devastating effect on the land.

Near the gasworks

For more than a hundred years coal has been used to make gas. This process takes place in gas works. But the land around disused gas works often contains high levels of poisons, such as arsenic and lead. Plants growing in the polluted soil draw in the poisons through their roots. Animals that eat the plants may be also be poisoned.

▼ *Houses were evacuated in Love Canal, USA, when it was discovered the land had been poisoned by dumped chemicals. People are still being compensated.*

Land that burns

In the 1950s a chemical company dumped containers of waste into an old canal near the Niagara Falls, USA. In the 1970s the canal was filled in and houses were built on top, but soon basements began to smell and children playing in their backyards found holes burnt in their shoes. Chemicals from the containers were seeping through the soil. Eventually the estate was evacuated. In 1980 a new law was introduced making companies responsible for their own waste.

▲ *The storage tank is all that remains of this gas works, but the ground may be contaminated for years to come.*

Power poison

In the 1950s people thought that nuclear power would replace coal and oil, and provide cheap, clean electricity. Around the world 25 countries developed nuclear **power stations**. But nuclear waste is radioactive and remains extremely dangerous for thousands of years.

France, the UK and the USA were nuclear power leaders. They planned to store their nuclear waste deep underground. Then they realized that earthquakes and accidents might one day cause leakages. Because of this, these countries stopped building new nuclear power stations. Other countries, such as China and South Korea, are still building new ones.

Making waste safe

Industries worldwide produce more than 400 million tonnes of poisonous waste each year. In 1992, 117 countries agreed to new laws that forced countries to process their waste safely. But this is expensive, so some companies pay poor countries to take in their poisonous waste for them. In 1998 Formosa Plastics in Taiwan sent waste to Cambodia. Hundreds of containers were dumped illegally near a town. Local people fled, but some died of poisoning. The waste was finally sent to the USA for processing.

Poisonous clouds

On 26 April 1986, the nuclear power station at Chernobyl, Ukraine, exploded. **Radioactive** clouds were blown across Europe, poisoning the land and air. About 10 000 people helping with the clean-up died. Even today local people are at serious risk from illnesses caused by **radiation**.

► *Pripyat in the Ukraine is a ghost city, abandoned after the nearby power station at Chernobyl exploded in 1986.*

Climate change

About 50 million years ago warm weather plants grew in the Arctic. Only half a million years ago ice sheets covered North America as far south as Kentucky.

Now the Earth is becoming warmer every year. In 1950 the average temperature was 13.86°C. By 1997 that had risen to 14.40°C. If the Earth continues to grow hotter at this rate, there will be more droughts, floods and fires in some parts of the world.

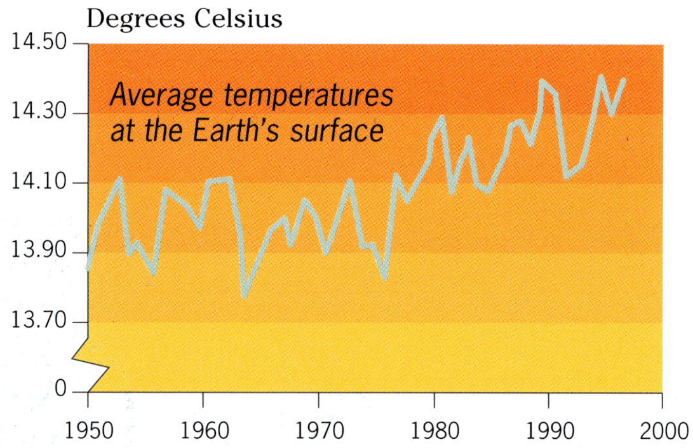

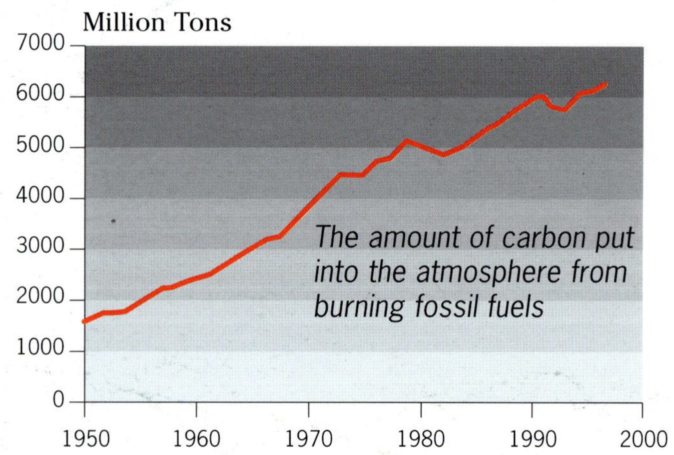

▲ *Glaciers are slow-moving rivers of ice. As the Earth becomes warmer, glaciers are melting. Those in the Alps have shrunk by half over the last 150 years.*

Fuelling climate change

About 30 per cent of the Sun's heat bounces off the Earth and is reflected back up again. Some of this heat is absorbed by gases in the atmosphere, which then give out heat. Over the last 200 years, air pollution has increased. Fertilizers, burning forests, cars, and power stations burning coal and oil all give out gases such as carbon dioxide, methane and nitrous oxide. These

◄ *These maps are based on figures for 1950 to 1997. Scientists believe that burning fossil fuels is one factor causing a steady rise in the Earth's temperature.*

are all known as **greenhouse gases**, and as they enter the atmosphere, more of the Sun's heat is absorbed, and the planet heats up. This effect is known as global warming.

Land underwater

As the Earth has become hotter, water in the oceans has warmed and expanded. Ice at the poles and on mountains has melted and flowed into the sea. As a result, the sea level has risen by about 20 centimetres in the last hundred years. People living on low-lying coasts and islands may be flooded more often as storms drive the rising sea over the land.

Flooding in Bangladesh

About 88 000 square kilometres of land along the coast of Bangladesh lies less than three metres above sea level. In 1970 the sea flooded much of this area, killing 266 000 people. In 50 years, if the sea continues to rise, a quarter of Bangladesh will lie permanently under water.

Drying out

About half the land on Earth is likely to become drier as the climate changes. The Great Plains of the USA, and the vast fields of the Ukraine, where much of the world's wheat is grown, are already suffering from drought. Wheat farming may have to move north and south towards the poles, where it is cooler.

Cooling it

Most countries sent representatives to the Climate Change Conference at Kyoto, Japan, in December 1997. They agreed to work towards reducing greenhouse gas emissions by burning less fossil fuels. Changes can be made at a local and national level. Cars can be banned from city areas and people can save energy in their homes. Power stations can use renewable energy sources. But saving energy on a wider scale would mean a drop in standards of living. Rich countries don't want this, and poorer countries feel it will stop them from developing. But all countries know that they must combat global warming.

▼ *Climate change is making dry grassland, such as the Steppes of Ukraine, even drier. The land is becoming less able to support crops and grazing cattle.*

Land in the future

Our future depends on everyone using land more carefully. We cannot expect it to provide food for us and space to live if we continue to turn land to desert and pollute it with chemicals.

▲ *Seed farms can supply many environments worldwide with different kinds of crop.*

Land to grow food

As the world population has grown, farmers have had to produce more food from the land. Chemical fertilizers help to increase harvests, but if overused they have less and less effect, and water running off fertilized fields can pollute rivers. A safer way to increase crops has been through plant breeding, using pollen from one type of plant to fertilize another. Thousands of new plants have been developed in this way. Despite this, good farmland is being built on, while unsuitable land such as semi-desert is being grazed or ploughed. The last wilderness areas are also being damaged by farming, mining and pollution.

▼ *This wilderness at Jabiluka, Australia, is threatened because the government is allowing uranium mining there. Local and international laws are needed to protect such land.*

▲ *An international treaty allows only scientific research stations in Antarctica.*

New crops

Sets of genes make every living thing unique. Scientists are now changing plant genes to develop **genetically modified** (GM) crops that can survive in difficult environments. For instance, fish genes have been added to tomatoes to create tomatoes that resist frost. Other plants will be able to kill their own pests. GM crops will help to produce more food, but no one knows what effect they will have on the environment, or on the humans who eat food made from them.

Traditional farming

Some farmers in the developed world are choosing to return to traditional ways of farming. They are suspicious of chemicals and new kinds of crop. They prefer to farm **organically**, using natural fertilizers on their crops and feeding animals with natural foods.

The untouched continent

Of the seven continents of the world, only Antarctica remains almost untouched. It lies around the South Pole and is mostly covered with ice. A wealth of minerals lies under the ice. In 1991 countries around the world agreed not to mine there for 50 years, because the area is important to scientists and researchers. If the minerals are needed in the future, pressure will grow to begin mining.

Holiday damage

Soon the biggest industry on Earth will be tourism. But large numbers of people travelling to the same place damages the land. Roads into parks can become jammed, and delicate footpaths become worn and littered with rubbish. On the other hand, tourism brings money to poor areas and may encourage a concern for the environment. The answer is to control tourism so that both the land and people benefit.

► *The Aceer rainforest reserve in Peru runs educational workshops to teach people about the rainforest.*

How you can help

Each of us changes the land around us, and can influence how land is used in other parts of the world. In our everyday lives there are things we can do to help improve the way the land is treated.

▲ *A compost heap converts kitchen waste into a natural fertilizer for plants.*

Don't bin it

Almost everything we buy in a supermarket comes in a box or bag. Then we put our purchases into more bags so we can carry them home. Manufacturing all this packaging uses up resources. And we usually do nothing with it but throw it away.

▼ *How much of this shopping will be thrown away?*

Recycle your rubbish

Save the packaging from one week's shopping and find out how much it weighs and how much space it takes up. Choose products that use less packaging, or packaging that can be recycled. Wherever possible buy items that have refills (such as shampoo or washing liquid) and reuse plastic bags to carry your shopping home. Sort out rubbish into paper products, cans, glass and plastic, and where possible, take them to a recycling centre.

Magic muck

Organic food is grown as part of a natural food cycle, where nutrients are put back into the soil using dung or **biodegradable** material rather than chemical fertilizers. Many shops sell organic food – but why not grow your own? Vegetables grown in gardens or pots can be fed with homemade compost. Do that and you will be part of the natural cycle.

Making compost

You can make your own compost quite easily. Some councils provide compost bins, or you can buy one, or make one by cutting the bottom off a plastic dustbin. Collect food waste and non-recyclable paper waste, such as kitchen towels, in different containers. (Scrunch the paper into small balls.) As they fill up, tip them into your compost bin. You can also add grass clippings, leaves and soil. The bin will soon become warm inside as the waste decays. When the compost looks rich and dark, after about four to six months, it is ready.

Working worms

Ideally your compost bin should stand on bare soil or grass, so that worms can wriggle in. If this isn't possible, you can buy composting kits. They come with special worms and small compost bins that can be kept in the kitchen or near the house.

▲ *Anything organic will make good compost. Collect different types of waste in containers and when they are full, tip them into your compost bin.*

Getting involved

All over the world people club together to change the way we use land. Non-governmental organizations (NGOs) tackle problems by telling politicians about problems and pressurizing them to make changes. Some help people improve their lives in simple ways; others work for the environment as a whole. NGOs give us all a chance to take action. You can help by becoming a member of one, or raising money to send. You'll find some useful addresses on pages 44–45 of this book.

Land projects

Here are three ways to find out about the land under your feet.

Your own landfill

To find out why a landfill is not an efficient way of disposing of rubbish, dig two holes in the ground side by side. Place something that will rot down, such as fruit, paper or vegetables in one hole. Put something non-biodegradable, such as a can or plastic wrapper in the other. Cover the rubbish with earth. (If you don't have a garden, bury your rubbish in pots and leave them outside.) After a week uncover the holes and see what has happened to the rubbish. Bury it again and wait for two months. What has happened to the rubbish now?

Landfill sites are used all over the world to dispose of our rubbish. But, as you will see, a lot of what we throw away will not disappear in the ground.

Living soil

On page 10 you can see a cross-section of soil. Why not find out what lives in the ground near you? You will need a spade, newspaper, a jar, and a sieve or colander.

Using a spade, make two parallel cuts in the soil about 10 centimetres apart, pushing the spade about 10 centimetres into the ground. Dig in the spade at both ends and lever out a box-shaped sample of soil. Place the soil on a newspaper and prise it apart with your hands, looking for worm-holes and the way roots have spread. Place any living creatures in a jar.

Sieve the soil to sort stones from the finer soil. Count the creatures, and divide them into different types: worms, insects; grubs, slugs and spiders, then return them to the ground. Imagine how much life there must be in a garden, or a park!

biodegradable waste

non-biodegradable waste

Wormery

Of all the creatures found in the soil, worms are especially valuable. They swallow leaves and earth, which pass through their bodies and enrich the soil with nutrients. Their tunnels also allow air to circulate.

You can buy wormeries made of two glass plates held closely together. The worms live in soil between them, and you can watch them tunnelling.

You can make your own wormery using two clean, clear plastic bottles, one a little fatter than the other. **1**. Cut the top off the bigger bottle; partly fill the thinner bottle with water, to keep the wormery stable and cool, and place it inside the bigger one. **2**. Pour some gravel into the space between the bottles. Then add layers of peat and sand, and finish with a layer of dead leaves.Collect some worms and put them on top of the leaves.

3. Wrap your wormery with dark plastic or cloth to keep out the light (but allow air in at the top) and put it somewhere cool and shady. Don't leave it indoors for more than a day or two. Every second day water the soil lightly and add more leaves, but don't let the soil become too wet. (Add holes to the bottom of the outer bottle to help drainage.) **4**. After two weeks see what has happened to the soil.

1

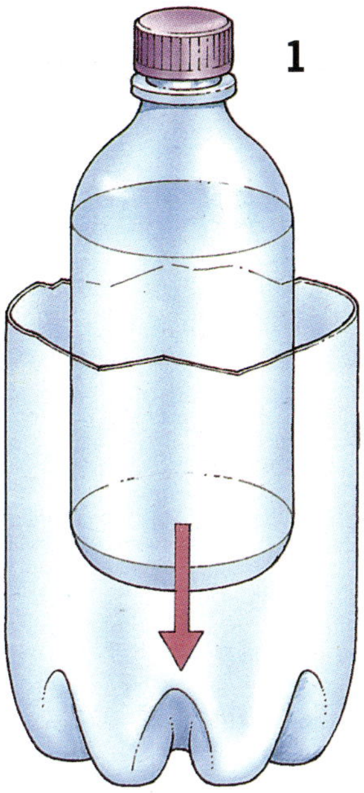

2

3

4

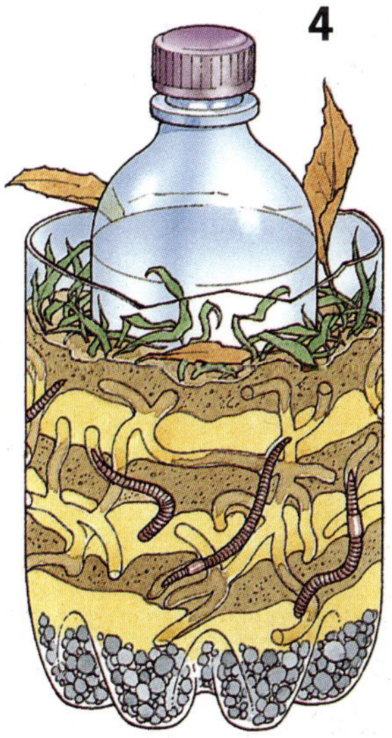

Land facts and figures

Less than a third of the Earth's surface is land, the rest is ocean. The land is divided into seven continents. Asia, the largest, occupies about a third of this area.

Highest, lowest, thickest thinnest...

The average height of the land above sea level is 860 metres. Of course, most places are either higher or lower, but Asia has both the highest and the lowest.

The world's highest place is the summit of Mount Everest (above). It is 8846 metres above sea level. The tallest mountain on Earth is Mauna Kea, on Hawaii. It is 10 205 metres tall, but most of this is below sea level. Only 4205 metres shows above the sea.

The shore around the Dead Sea, between Israel and Jordan, is the lowest place on Earth, 400 metres below sea level. The water that collects in this lake can't escape, but slowly evaporates. Minerals have built up in the water to such an extent that fish cannot live there.

Under the oceans, the Earth's crust is an average of six kilometres deep. On dry land it is thicker, averaging about 35 kilometres. In Asia, where the crust has been folded to form the Himalaya Mountains, it is 80 kilometres thick in places. But in the central valley of California, USA, the crust is only 20 kilometres thick.

No one has dug completely through the Earth's crust. The deepest mines reach only four kilometres down. Russian scientists who drilled down 15 kilometres to investigate the crust were not even half way through.

Your own patch of land

More than half of the people in the world live in Asia, and 30 per cent of those live in China, where there are about 125 Chinese to every square kilometre. Europe has an average of more than 300 people to each square kilometre. In contrast, large areas of North Africa and Canada have less than one person for every square kilometre. Cities occupy the most crowded land. Many cities in the developing world are growing by up to half a million people every year.

Bombay is the largest city in India, and the fastest growing city in the world. It is built on islands, so it cannot easily expand outwards. The city's 103 square kilometres of land are home to 17 million people, which is about 165 000 people to every square kilometre of land.

Dry land

Deserts cover about 33 per cent of all land. They occur where there is less than 25 centimetres of rain in a year. Only a few plants and animals can survive, and the land is mostly stone or sand.

The Gobi Desert in Asia lies on a vast plateau, a plain more than 1000 metres high, and covers an area of 1 295 000 square kilometres. Its name is Mongolian for 'place without water'. The weather is warm rather than hot, and there are areas where water collects, and where streams disappear into the sand.

The Sahara Desert (left), in Africa, is the largest desert in the world, covering an area of about nine million square kilometres – the size of the USA. It is a hot desert, with areas of high mountains and sand dunes, but across much of it there are enough plants for nomads to survive, grazing their sheep and goats.

Land around the globe

How people use land is affected by the natural environment. By looking at these maps you can see where the largest populations are, and compare human land use with the land's natural vegetation.

Large stretches of land are sparsely populated. These areas, such as in central Asia or along northern edges of Asia, are covered with forest, desert or tundra. In areas where there are more people, the land has usually been changed far more. In the USA, arable farming has replaced open grassland. Most of northern Europe's natural forest has been cut down. In huge cities, land is used for houses, businesses, schools and roads, while the surrounding area is used to produce people's food.

Population distribution around the world

▼ *Most land on Earth is thinly populated. The most densely populated areas are in Europe, India, Pakistan, China and the USA.*

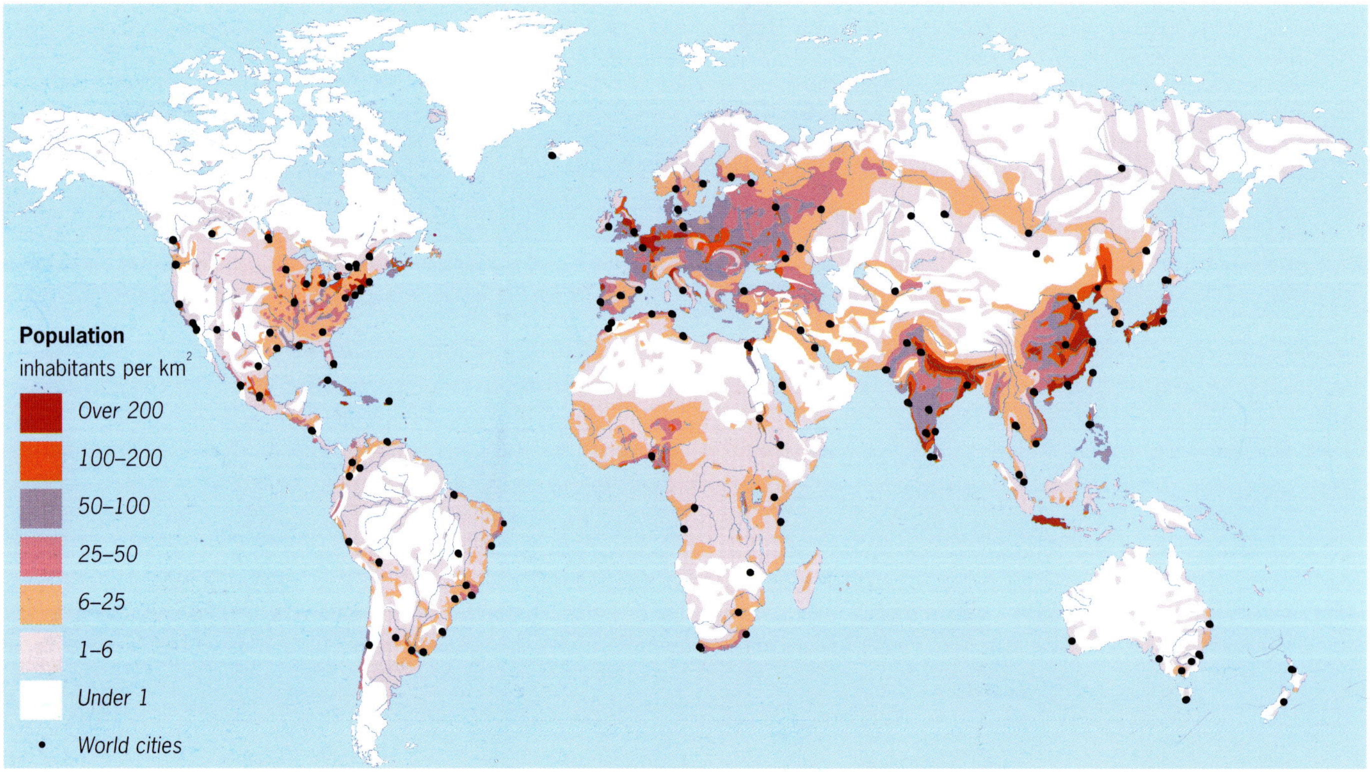

Human land use around the world

▼ *Where there are large populations, land has to produce lots of food. Elsewhere, most land is non-productive, forested, or used for rough grazing.*

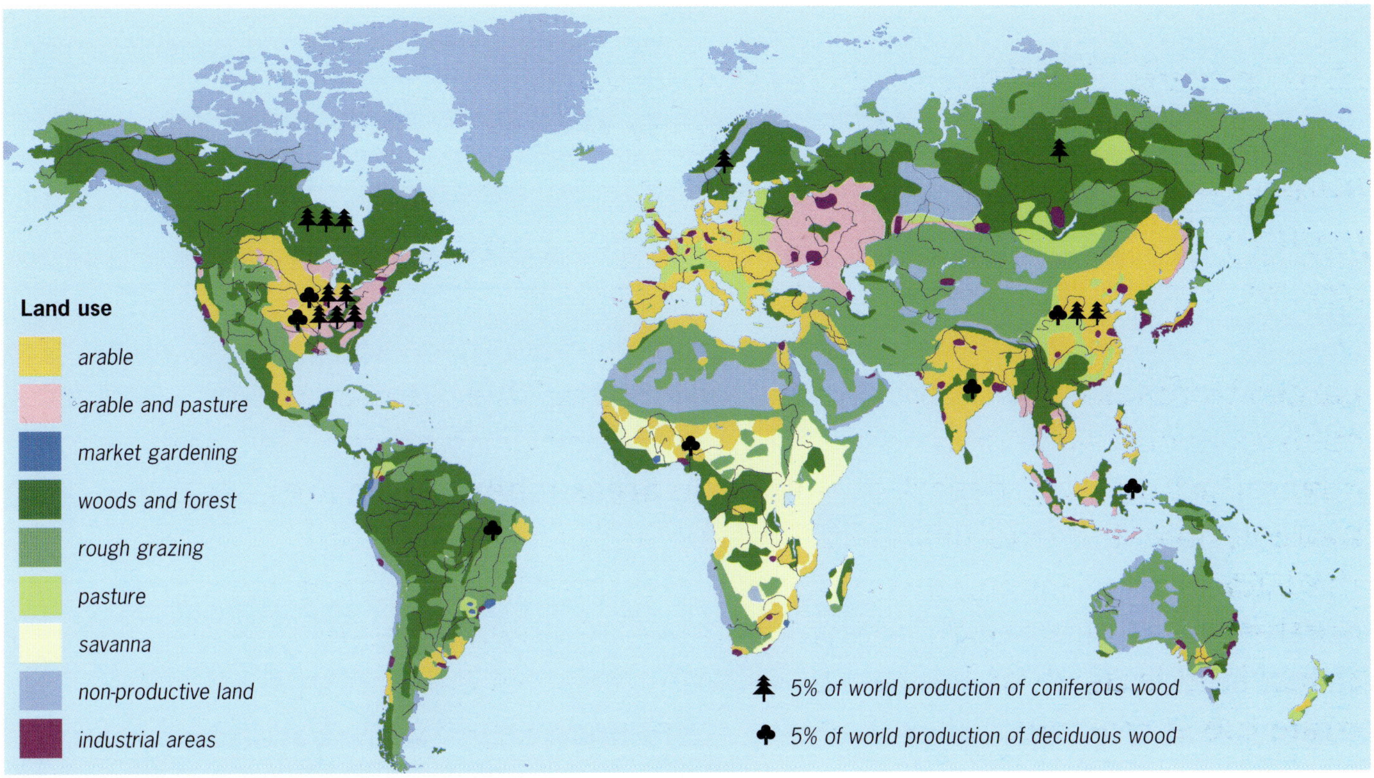

Natural vegetation around the world

▼ *This map shows the plant eco-systems that would naturally cover the land. People have changed these over thousands of years, reducing the forests, plains and wetlands.*

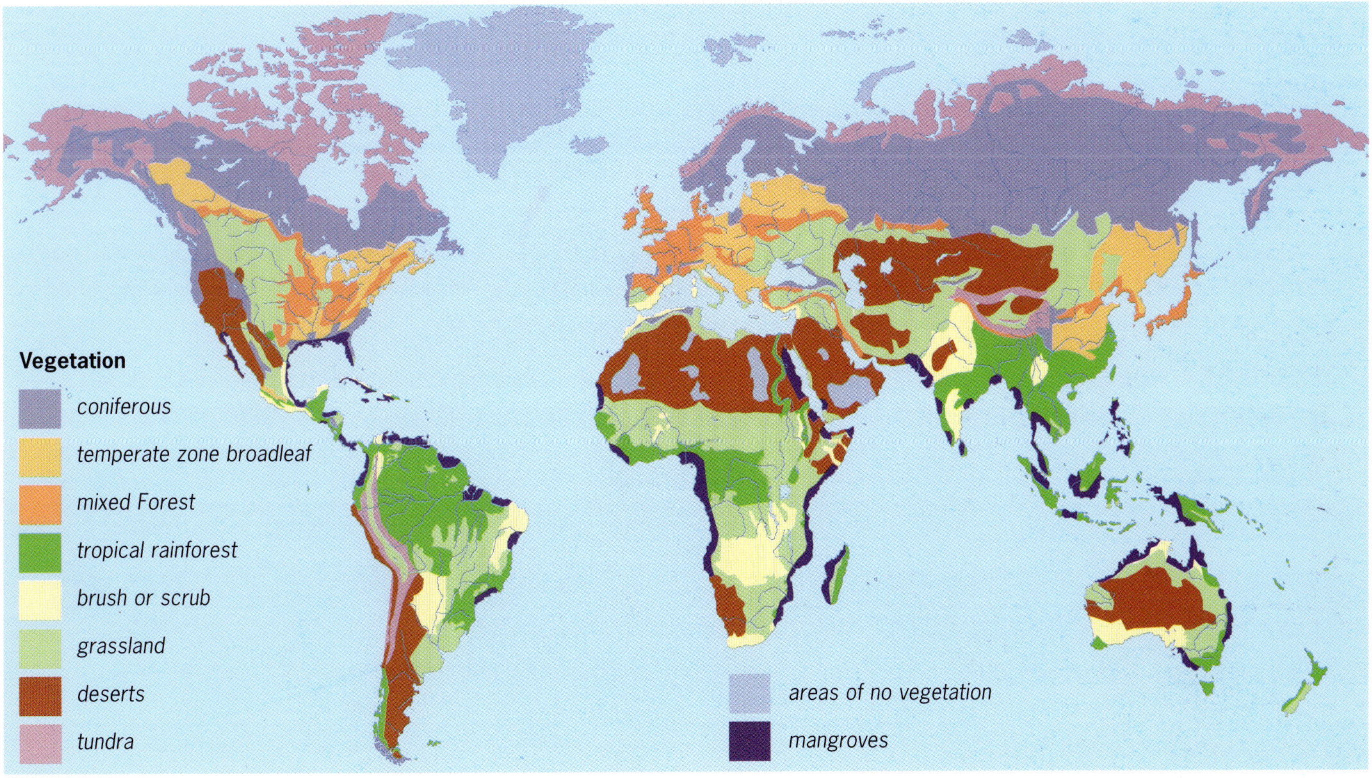

Further information

Many organizations will supply information about various aspects of land and the environment. You can find out more by looking into their websites, or sending a large stamped addressed envelope for their latest project news.

▲ *Volunteer conservation workers help to build and improve trails through the Ruwenzori Mountains in Africa.*

WORLDWIDE AID (NGOs)

Actionaid works with the poor in many developing countries, including projects to help farmers improve their land and livestock.
PO Box 100, London SE1 7RT
http://www.oneworld.org/actionaid

Christian Aid Amongst its many activities Christian Aid supports people who lose their land through environmental disasters.
PO Box 100, London SE1 7RT
www.christian-aid.org.uk

Friends of the Earth (FoE) is the largest network of environmental groups in the world. Its quarterly magazine *Earth Matters* includes news of environmental campaigns.
26-28 Underwood Street, London N1 7JQ
http://www.foe.co.uk

Greenpeace aims to stop further destruction and pollution of the land.
Canonbury Villas, London N1 2PN
http://www.greenpeace.org.uk/greenbytes

Oxfam helps people worldwide to improve their lives without harming the environment. They produce their own education catalogue.
274 Banbury Road, Oxford OX2 7DX
http://www.oxfam. org. uk

LAND IN THE UK

Rainforest Concern deals with all issues concerning the protection of the world's rainforests.
27 Lansdowne Crescent, London W11 2NS
www.rainforest.org.uk

The Centre for Alternative Technology explores ways of managing the land, and gives advice on how to make perfect compost.
Machynlleth, Powys, SW20 9AZ
www.cat.org.uk

The Earth Centre is a visitor centre giving advice on sustainable living and how we can be more environmentally friendly. Denaby Main, Conisborough, Doncaster, South Yorkshire, DN12 4EA

The Environment Agency is the government information service for England and Wales: Rio House, Waterside Drive, Aztec West, Almondsbury, Bristol BS12 4UD

Henry Doubleday Research Association provides a free information pack on organic gardening in the UK and practical projects in the developing countries.

▼ *Aid arrives for people in the Sudan, whose homes and land have been flooded.*

The Soil Association stresses the connections between soil, plants, animals and people, and promotes organic farming. Look out for organic food that bears the Soil Association foodmark. Members receive the magazine *Living Earth*, and offers on books and information packs. Bristol House, 40-56 Victoria Street, Bristol BS1 6BY. www.soilassociation.org

Waste Watch Wasteline provides information on what can and cannot be recycled. Tel: 0171-248-0242.

Further reading

The Atlas of Endangered Resources by Steve Pollock (Belitha Press, 1995)

Don't Burn It or Bury It (Friends of the Earth)

Eat Organic (Soil association)

Kingfisher Young Discoverers: *Rubbish and Recycling*, *Pollution and Waste* (Kingfisher Books)

Land Ecology by Jennifer Cochrane (Wayland, 1987)

Local Food for Local People (Soil Association)

Muck and Magic by Jo Readman, gives advice on starting your own organic garden (Soil Association)

Protecting Our Planet: Fuels for the Future by Steve Parker (Wayland 1997)

Protecting Our Planet: Forests for Life by Edward Parker (Wayland 1997)

Protecting Our Planet: Waste, Recycling and Re-use by John Baines (Wayland 1997)

Protecting Our Planet: The World's Wild Places by John Howson (Wayland 1997)

Glossary

artificial fertilizer A manmade mixture of chemicals used to feed plants.

bacteria Tiny living things that help to break down dead plants and animals.

biodegradable Anything that can be broken down by bacteria, such as dead plants and animals.

carbon dioxide A gas that makes up about 0.4 per cent of the air, but is increasing. It is the main greenhouse gas.

cash crops Food plants grown to be sold and sent away, rather than be eaten locally.

compost A mixture of rotted plants and other organic matter that improves the soil and provides food for plants.

conservation treaty An agreement between countries to look after certain parts of the natural world.

decay The process that breaks up plants and animals after they have died.

developed countries Countries, mainly in Europe, North America and Australasia, that have become wealthy through the growth of industries, trade and banks.

environment The surroundings in which people, animals and plants live.

erosion The wearing away of land by weather, and water in all its forms – seas, rivers, rain and ice.

fossil fuels Fuels, including coal, gas and oil, formed millions of years ago from the remains of plants. When burnt, the carbon in those plants is released as carbon dioxide and other gases.

genetically modified (GM) Plants and animals that have been changed by having their genes (the parts that give them their individual characteristics) altered.

global warming An increase in the Earth's surface temperature caused by an increase in carbon dioxide and other greenhouse gases in the atmosphere.

greenhouse gases Gases in the air that store heat from the sun. The more of these gases there are in the air, the greater the amount of heat stored. The main greenhouse gases are carbon monoxide, carbon dioxide, methane and nitrous oxide.

groundwater Water lying underground, such as rain that has seeped into the rocks.

habitat The natural home of a plant or animal.

humus The decayed bits of plant and animal in the soil that provides food for new plants.

igneous rock Rocks that are cooled, solidified magma, either from volcanoes or beneath the surface of the land.

irrigation Watering the land using manmade canals, pipes and ditches.

landfill holes in the ground into which rubbish is tipped.

loess A rich soil, good for plants, made up of fine dust blown by the wind.

magma The molten material that lies below the Earth's crust, and which erupts from volcanoes.

metamorphic rock Rocks that were once either sedimentary or igneous, but have been changed by heat, pressure or water.

minerals Natural material found in the ground, such as iron, that is not living and does not come from animals or plants.

monoculture A type of farming where a single crop is grown every year.

monsoon A wind that brings heavy rain. The strongest blows from the Indian Ocean in summer, bringing rains to southern Asia.

natural resource Something that occurs naturally that can be used by humans.

nitrogen The main gas in the air, making up about 78 per cent.

nutrients Simple chemicals that provide food for plants and animals. Plants take up nutrients through their roots.

organic Coming from a living thing. Now also used to describe food that has been produced **organically** in a natural way, without artificial fertilizers.

organism Any living thing.

parent rock The rock under a soil that affects what kind of soil is formed.

particles The tiny pieces left when any material breaks up or is eroded.

plains large areas of mainly flat and often low-lying land.

plateau An area of flat land that is high above sea level.

pollution The result of anything that poisons or harms the environment.

power station A place where electricity is made, using fuels such as coal or oil, or other forms of energy such as wind.

radiation A form of energy given off by **radioactive** material. Large doses of radiation can kill animals and plants.

raw materials Any mineral, rock, animal or plant that is used to make something.

seam A thin layer of rock or mineral that can be mined, such as coal.

sediment Bits of rock or plant that settle to the bottom of rivers, lakes or seas.

sedimentary rock Rock made up of sediment that collected underwater millions of years ago.

weathering The breaking up of rocks by wind, water and sun.

wetlands Any land that is regularly waterlogged or underwater, such as marshes and mangrove swamps.

wilderness Land untouched by humans.

Index